SRIMAD BHAGAVAD GITHA
4.Jnana Yogaha

JET Publisnıng House

INDIA   USA

TOWARDS EXCELLENCE

P
R
A
J
N
A

Title	SRIMAD BHAGAVAD GITHA
Subtitle	Jnana Yogaha
Copyright	Jeeyar Educational Trust
First Edition	2018
Contributor	His Holiness Chinna Jeeyar Swamiji

CONTACT US:

INDIA

JIVA
Sriramanagaram, Shamshabad,
R.R. Dist. Andhra Pradesh - 509 325
Phone: 95535 49971, 95535 499

UNITED STATES

JETUSA Inc.
Jeeyar Asram, 222, Dey Road,
CRANBURY, NJ 08512, USA
Phone:609-297-8797

Website: www.prajna4me.org   Email: prajna@jetusa.org

Jai Srimannarayana !

Dear Blessed Children of God !

It is wonderful that you are learning Bhagavad Gi:tha. This is, in fact, greatly relevant to your life. You can discuss about various topics of time tested scientific facts, and Universal truths; you can implement them on all occassions possible. Yes! It makes your life brave and brighter!!!

PRAJNA of JET USA is opening up an opportunity to you, to discover the secrets of our ancient history. Bhagavad Gi:tha is a nice beginning to unlock your inner "Prajna". With its divine vibrations, we are sure that you will achieve your dreams and excel in your life along with your friends!

Enjoy and experience the Divine Glory of Bhagavad Gi:tha. Our Mangalasasanams to you all!

Jai Srimannarayana !

Sri Krushna Parabramhane: Namaha

SRIMAD BHAGAVAD GI:THA:

AN INTRODUCTION

Jai Srimannarayana !

Human life is blessed with a great amount of knowledge. This knowledge allows him to discover the truths of the Nature around and also the secrets of the self. Not just being satisfied with what is experienced through the senses, human knowledge can penetrate to the deeper levels of this seen world. That journey from seen to unseen, opened up the doors to understand that everything in this world is multi-dimensional, but we are so far able to discover only a few of them.

That understanding went in two directions. Externally, it has gone beyond the planets and stars, trying to know about the origin of these galaxies and non-matter around. Internally, it is exploring the cell, the gene, the life and the soul itself. Of course, the journey, the quest for the Truth, started long ago and it is still going on and on revealing many wonders of this mysterious Creation.

We have far advanced science based on some pragmatic evidences following the theoretical concepts. However, Vedic seers made a holistic approach about the whole existence of the inner as well as outer worlds. And they explained from 'unseen to the seen', rather than from 'seen to the unseen'. They brought down the facts as how these things happened and when they have started, the purpose of these objects that are around. Man is not able to exactly understand all the truths, due to his limitated perception. So, whatever is not seen or not been able to prove, was named after philosophy. But, Philosophy is just another dimension of what we call science today. There are other dimensions which the Vedas and Vedic literature, are trying to explain.

The Vedas are so many, as it is said, ' Anantha: vai Ve:da:ha'. And hence, we cannot go through the whole Vedic literature to understand the essence of it. The Lord Krishna revealed such essence of the Vedas, to his disciple Arjuna, which came to be known as Bhagavad Gi:tha. Though that celestial song superficially shows how Arjuna was in dilemma whether to fight or not and how Lord Krishna was trying to put him in action by His preaching.

But, it is for a seeker, to a common human, who always lands in a dilemma while executing his duties, whether to do or not to do, and while doing so, how to do and how not to do, what to expect and what not to expect, and so on. The celestial song Bhagavad Githa reveals the process of keeping Man in proper action supported by right knowledge not only to break down the past karmic bondage, but also to protect him from the results of new karmas. Bhagavadgitha also enlightens man, with his limitations, while he is striving for blissful state.

A brief purport with the meanings of the words, is presented to each Slo:ka to help the beginners for better understanding. Interpretations may vary depending on the school of thought the commentator follows, but the teaching of the Lord in the form of slo:kas will never change. For easy understanding of the meaning, sanskrit words were kept in an order, as the english sentences are formed. Most common practice in understanding the purport of a sanskrit slo:ka is to collect all the meanings of the words and form sentences. That has been modified here. We are sure that the reader may find it while going throug the text.

For the readers' convenience a few indications were provided in the transliterated form of sanksrit slo:kas, to have perfect chanting, while avoiding complications.

A vowel without any mark becomes a short vowel by default. The mark " : " after a vowel, should be pronounced as a long vowel. There are some intricate syllables like tha ttha, da, dha, tta etc. Though those sounds were represented to the closer vicinity of the sanskrit letter, yet, the reader may listen to the voice and then find the accurate pronunciation.

Our Mangalasasanams to all the readers to use it well in understanding and practising the message graced by Lord Krishna.

Jai Srimannarayana !

PRAJNA PLEDGE

Jai Srimannarayana!

O Mother Earth! I, being your best child and responsible citizen of this world, take this pledge!

I shall revere my parents, my family, my Gurus and treat everyone with love.

I shell serve my community, my country and those in need.

I pledge to protect the Nature by caring for animals, trees and the environment.

I will learn from the experiences of my ancestors and pass it on to future generations.

I, as student of Prajna, swear to abide by the universal commandments.

Worship your own and Respect all &
Serve all beings as service to God.
         Jai Srimannarayana!

Telugu	Hindi	English	Telugu	Hindi	English
అ	अ	a	ట	ट	ta
ఆ	आ	a:	ఠ	ठ	tta
ఇ	इ	i	డ	ड	**tta**
ఈ	ई	i:	ఢ	ढ	**da**
ఉ	उ	u	ఢ	ड़	**dda**
ఊ	ऊ	u:	ణ	ढ़	**dha**
ఋ	ऋ	ru	ణ	ण	**na**
ౠ	ॠ	ru:	త	त	tha
ఌ	अलु	lu	త్త	त्त	ththa
ౡ	अलू	lu:	థ	थ ⎱ ⎰	ttha
ఎ		e	ద	द	da
ఏ	ए	e:	ద్ద	द्द	dda
ఐ	ऐ	ai	ధ	ध	dha
ఒ		o	న	न	na
ఓ	ओ	o:	ప	प	pa
ఔ	औ	au/ow	ఫ	फ	pha
అం	अं	am	బ	ब	ba
అః	अः	aha	భ	भ	bha
క	क	ka	మ	म	ma
ఖ	ख	kha	య	य	ya
గ	ग	ga	ర	र	ra
ఘ	घ	gha	ల	ल	la
ఙ	ङ	nga	వ	व	va
చ	च	cha	శ	श	sa
ఛ	च	chcha	ష	ष	sha
ఛ	छ ⎱ ⎰	chha	స	स	sa
ఛ	छ		హ	ह	ha
జ	ज	ja	ళ	ळ	la
ఝ	झ	jha	ఱ		rra
ఞ	ञ	ini	క్ష	क्ष	ksha
			జ్ఞ		Jna

● This letter comes only in the middle of the word

● ● This letter comes in the beginning/middle of the word

☞ Pronounciation of both these letters is almost similar

Guruparampara

srisaile:sa daya: pa:thram
dhi:bhakthya:di guna:rnavam|
yathi:ndra pravanam vande:
ramya ja:ma:tharam munim || 1

lakshmi: na:ttha sama:rambha:m
na:ttha ya:muna madhyama:m |
asmad a:cha:rya paryantha:m
vande: guru parampara:m || 2

yo: nithyam achyutha pada:mbuja yugma rukma
vya:mo:hathas thadithara:ni thruna:ya me:ne:|
asmadguro:r bhagavatho:sya dayaika sindho:ho
ra:ma:nujasya charanau saranam prapadye:|| 3

ma:tha: pitha: yuvathayas thanaya: vibhu:thihi
sarvam yade:va niyame:na madanvaya:na:m |
a:dyasya nah kulapathe:r vakula:bhira:mam
sri:math thadanghri yugalam pranama:mi mu:rdhna: || 4

bhu:tham saras cha mahada:hvaya bhattana:ttha
sri: bhakthi sa:ra kulase:khara yo:giva:ha:n |
bhaktha:nghri renu paraka:la yathi:ndra misra:n
srimath para:nkusa munim pranatho:smi nithyam || 5

Gi:tha:dhya:nam (Invocation)

sukla:mbara dharam vishnum
sasi varnam chathur bhujam |
prasanna vadanam dhya:ye:th
sarva vighno:pasa:nthaye: || 1

yasya dvirada vakthra:dya:ha
pa:rishadya:h paras satham |
vighnam nighnathi sathatham
vishvakse:nam thama:sraye: || 2

vya:sam vasi:shtta naptha:ram
sakthe:h pauthram akalmasham |
para:sara:thmajam vande:
sukatha:tham thapo:nidhim || 3

samyang nya:ya kala:pe:na
mahatha: bha:rathe:na cha |
upa brumhitha ve:da:ya
namo: vya:sa:ya vishnave: || 4

sa:radhyam arjunasya:jau
kurvan gi:tha:mrutham dadau |
lo:kathrayo:paka:ra:ya
thasmai krushna:thamane: namaha || 5

prapanna pa:rija:tha:ya
ve:thra tho:thraika pa:naye: |
jna:na mudra:ya krushna:ya
gi:thamrutha duhe: namaha || 6

kara kamala nidarsitha:thma mudraha
parikalitho:nnatha barhi barha chu:daha |
ithara kara gruhi:tha ve:thra tho:thro:
mama hrudi sannidhim a:thano:thu saurihi || 7

agre: kruthva: kamapi charanam ja:nu naike:na thishtan
pascha:th pa:rtham pranaya sajusha: chakshusha: vi:kshama:naha |
savye: tho:thram kara sarasije: dakshine: jna:na mudra:m
a:bibhra:no: ratham adhivasan pa:thunas su:tha ve:shaha || **8**

krushnam kamala pathra:ksham punya sravana ki:rthanam |
va:sude:vam jagad yo:nim naumi narayanam harim || 9

krushna:ya ya:dave:ndra:ya
jna:na mudra:ya yo:gine: |
na:tha:ya rukmini:sa:ya
namo: ve:da:ntha ve:dine: || 10

CLASS BEGINNING SLOKAS

O:m asmad gurubhyo: namaha |

O:m namah parama rushibhyo:
namah parama rushibhyaha | (2 times)

O:m! pu:rnamidam pu:rnamadaha
pu:rna:th pu:rnamudachyathe: |
pu:rnasya pu:rnama:da:ya
pu:rname:va:vasishyathe: || O:m!

O:m! i:sa:va:syamidagum sarvam
yath kincha jagathya:m jagath |
the:na thyakthe:na bhunji:ttha:ha
ma: grudhah kasyasviddhanam || O:m!

ka:syapa:nvaya sanja:tham na:ra:yana pada:sritham
sri:man na:ra:yanam vande: yathi:swara sriya:jusham ||

CLASS ENDING SLOKAS

O:m! agne:! naya supattha: ra:ye: asma:n
viswa:ni de:va! vayuna:ni vidwa:n |
yuyo:dhyasmath juhura:na me:naha
bhu:yishtta:nthe: nama ukthim vidhe:ma || O:m!

O:m! pu:rnamidam pu:rnamadaha
pu:rna:th pu:rnamudachyathe: |
pu:rnasya pu:rnama:da:ya
pu:rname:va:vasishyathe: || O:m!

O:m namah parama rushibhyo:
namah parama rushibhyaha | (2 times)

O:m asmad gurubhyo: namaha |

Jai Srimannarayana!

SRI:MAD BHAGAVAD GI:TA:

o:m asmath gurubhyo: namaha

Attha Chathurttho:dhya:yaha (Jna:na Yo:gaha)

sri: bhagava:n uva:cha
imam vivaswathe: yo:gam
pro:kthava:n aham avyayam |
vivaswa:n manave: pra:ha
manur ikshwa:kave:bravi:th || 1

e:vam parampara: pra:ptham
imam ra:jarshayo: viduhu |
sa ka:le:ne:ha mahatha:
yo:go: nashtah paranthapa! || 2

sa e:va:yam maya: the::dya
yo:gah pro:kthah pura:thanaha
bhaktho::si me: sakha: che:thi
rahasyam hye:thad uththamam   3

Arjuna uva:cha
avaram bhavatho: janma
param janma vivaswathaha |
kattham e:thad vija:ni:ya:m
thwam a:dau pro:kthava:n ithi   4

sri: bhagava:n uva:cha
bahu:ni me: vyathi:tha:ni
janma:ni thava cha:rjuna ! |
tha:nyaham ve:da sarva**ni**
na thwam ve:tthha paramthapa! || 5

ajo::pi sannavyaya:thma:
bhu:tha:na:m i:**s**waro::pisan |
prakruthim swa:m adhish**tt**a:ya
sambhava:my a:thma ma:yaya: || 6

yada: yada: hi dharmasya
gla:nir bhavathi bha:ratha! |
abhyuttha:nam adharmasya

thada:thma:nam sruja:myaham || 7

parithra:**n**a:ya sa:dhu:na:m
vina:**s**a:ya cha dushkrutha:m |
dharma samsttha:pana:rttha:ya
sambhava:mi yuge: yuge: || 8

janma karma cha me: divyam
e:vam yo: ve:ththi thaththwathaha |
thyakthwa: de:ham punarjanma
naithi ma:m e:thi so::rjuna! || 9

vi:tha ra:ga bha:yakro:dha:ha
manmaya: ma:m upa:**s**ritha:ha |
bahavo: jna:na thapasa:
pu:tha: madbha:vam a:gatha:ha || 10

ye: yattha: ma:m prapadyanthe:
tha:ms thaththaiva bhaja:my aham |
mama varthma: nuvarthanthe:
manushya:h pa:rttha! sarva**s**aha || 11

ka:nkshanthah karma**n**a:m siddhim
yajantha iha de:vatha:ha |
kshipram hi ma:nushe: lo:ke:
siddhir bhavathi karmaja: || 12

cha:thur var**n**yam maya: srushtam
gu**n**a karma vibha:ga**s**aha|
thasya kartha:ram api ma:m
viddhyakartha:ram avyayam || 13

na ma:m karma:**n**i limpanthi
na me: karmaphale: spruha: |
ithi ma:m yo:bhija:na:thi

karmabhir na sa baddhyathe: || 14

e:vam jna:thwa: krutham karma
pu:rvair api mumukshubhihi |
kuru karmaiva thasma:th thwam
pu:rvaih pu:rvatharam krutham || 15

kim karma kim akarme:thi
kavayo::py athra mo:hitha:ha |
thath the: karma pravakshya:mi
yad jna:thwa: mo:kshyase::subha:th || 16

karmano: hyapi bo:ddhavyam
bo:ddhavyam cha vikarmanaha |
akarmanas cha bo:ddhavyam
gahana: karmano: gathihi || 17

karmany akarma yah pasye:th
akarmani cha karma yaha |
sa buddhima:n manushye:shu
sa yukthah kruthsna karmakruth || 18

yasya sarve: sama:rambha:ha
ka:masankalpa varjitha:ha |
jna:na:gni dagdha karma:nam
tham a:huhu panditham budha:ha || 19

thyakthwa: karma phala:sangam
nithyathruptho: nira:srayaha |
karmany abhi pravruththo:pi
naiva kimchith karo:thi saha || 20

nira:si:r yatha chiththa:thma:
thyaktha sarvwa parigrahaha |
sa:ri:ram ke:valam karma
kurvann a:pno:thi kilbisham || 21

yadruchha: la:bha santhushto:
dwandwa:thi:tho: vimathsaraha |
samas siddha:va siddhau cha
kruthwa::pi na nibaddhyathe: || 22

gathasangasya mukthasya
jna:na:vastthitha che:thasaha |
yajna: ya:charathah karma
samagram pravili:yathe: || 23

bramh:arpanam bramhahavihi
bramha:gnau bramhana: hutham |
bramhaiva the:na ganthavyam
bramha karma sama:dhina: || 24

daivam e:va:pare: yajnam
yo:ginah paryupa:sathe: |
bramha:gna:vapare: yajnam
yajne: naivo:pa juhwathi || 25

sro:thra:di:n indriya:ny anye:
samyam a:gnishu juhwathi |
sabda:di:n vishaya:n anye:
indriya:gnishu juhwathi || 26

sarva:ni:ndriya karma:ni
pra:na karma:ni cha:pare: |
a:thma samyama yo:ga:gnau
juhwathi jna:na di:pithe: || 27

dravya yajna:s thapo: yajna:ha
yo:gayajna:s thattha:pare: |
sva:dhya:ya jna:na yajna:s cha
yathayas samsritha vratha:ha || 28

apa:ne: juhwathi pra:nam
pra:ne:: pa:nam thattha::pare: |
pra:na::pa:na gathi:ruddhwa:
pra:na:ya:ma para:yana:ha || 29

apare: niyatha:ha:ra:ha
pra:na:n pra:ne:shu juhwathi |
sarve::py e:the: yajnavido:
yajna kshapitha kalmasha:ha || 30

yajna sishta:mrutha bhujo:
ya:nthi bramha sana:thanam |

na:yam lo:ko::sthya yajnasya
kutho:nyah kurusaththama ! || 31

e:vam bahuvidha: yajna:ha
vithatha:h brahma**n**o: mukhe: |
karmaja:n viddhi tha:n sarva:n
e:vam jna:thwa: vimo:kshyase: || 32

sre:ya:n dravyamaya:d yajna:th
jna:na yajnah paranthapa! |
sarvam karma:khi:lam pa:rttha!
jna:ne: parisama:pyathe: || 33

thadwiddhi pra**n**ipa:the:na
paripra**s**ne:na se:vaya: |
upade:kshyanthi the: jna:nam
jna:ninas thaththwadar**s**inaha || 34

yath jna:thwa na punarmo:ham
e:vam ya:syasi pa:**nd**ava! |
ye:na bhu:tha:nya**s**e:she:**n**a
drakshyasy a:thman yattho: mayi || 35

api che:d asi pa:pe:bhyaha
sarve:bhyaha pa:pakruththamaha |
sarvam jna:na plave:naiva
vrujinam santharishyasi || 36

yatthaidha:msi samiddho::gnihi
bhasmasa:th kuruthe::rjuna ! |
jna:na:gnis sarva karma:ni

bhasmasa:th kuruthe: thattha: || 37

nahi jna:ne:na sadrusam
pavithram iha vidyathe: |
thathsvayam yo:ga samsiddhaha
ka:le:na::thmani vindathi || 38

sraddha:va:n labhathe: yo:gam
thath paras samyathe:ndriyaha |
jna:nam labdhwa: para:m **s**a:nthim
achire:**n** a:dhi gachhathi || 39

ajna**s**cha: **s**raddha dha:na**s**cha
samsaya:thma: vina**s**yathi |
na:yam lo:ko::sthi na paro:
na sukham sam**s**aya:thmanaha || 40

yo:ga sannyastha karma:nam
jna:na sanchanna samsayam |
a:thmavantham na karma:ni
nibadhnanthi dhananjaya! || 41

thasma:d ajna:na sambhu:tham
hruthsttham jna:na:sin a::thmanaha |
chhithvainam samsayam yo:gam
a:thishtto:th thishtta bha:ratha! || 42

ithi srimad bhagavadgi:tha:su upanishathsu brahma vidya:ya:m yo:gasa:sthre: sri krushna:rjuna samva:de: jna:na yo:go: na:ma chathurttho:dhya:yaha ||

Thus concluded the 4th chapter 'Jnana Yogaha' of Sri:mad Bhagavad Gi:tha, an Upanishath, a Bramha Vidya, a Yo:gasa:sthra and this is a dialogue between Sri Krushna & Arjuna.

sri:krushna parabramhane: namaha
sarvam sri: krushna:rpanam asthu

Concluding prayer

gi:tha: sa:sthram idam punyam
yah patte:th prayathah puma:n |
vishno:h padam ava:pno:thi
bhaya so:ka:di varjithaha || 1

gi:tha:dhyayana si:lasya
pra:na:ya:ma parasya cha |
naiva santhi hi pa:pa:ni
pu:rva janma krutha:ni cha || 2

mala nirmo:chanam pumsa:m
jala sna:nam dine: dine: |
sakrud gi:tha:mbhasi sna:nam
samsa:ra mala mo:chanam || 3

gi:tha: sugi:tha: karthavya:
kimanyais sa:sthra sangrahaihi |
ya: swayam padmana:bhasya
mukha padma:d vinissrutha: || 4

bha:ratha:mrutha sarvasvam
vishno:r vakthra:d vinissrutham |
gi:tha: gango:dakam pi:thwa:
punar janma na vidyathe: || 5

sarvo:panishado: ga:vaha
do:gdha: go:pa:la nandanaha |
pa:rttho: vathsas sudhi:r bho:ktha:
dugdham gi:tha:mrutham mahath|| 6

e:kam sa:sthram de:vaki: puthra gi:tham
e:ko: de:vo: de:vaki: puthra e:va |
e:ko: manthras thasya na:ma:ni ya:ni
karma:pye:kam thasya de:vasya se:va || 7

ka:ye:na va:cha: manase:ndriyair va:
buddhya:thmana: va: prakruthe:s swabha:va:th |
karo:mi yadyath sakalam parasmai
na:ra:yana:ye:thi samarpaya:mi || 8

srimanna:ra:yana:ye:thi samarpaya:mi sarvam
srikrushna:rpanam asthu

o:m asmath gurubhyo: namaha

Jna:na Yo:gaha

SLOKA-1

sri: bhagava:n uva:cha
imam vivaswathe: yo:gam
pro:kthava:n aham avyayam |
vivaswa:n manave: pra:ha
manur ikshwa:kave:bravi:th || 1

Word Split

imam – vivaswathe: – yo:gam
pro:kthava:n – aham – avyayam |
vivaswa:n – manave: – pra:ha
manuhu – ikshwakave: – abravi:th ||

Meaning

sri: bhagavan	=	*The Lord*
uva:cha	=	*said*
aham	=	I
pro:kthava:n	=	taught
imam	=	this
avyayam	=	imperishable
yo:gam	=	*karma yo:ga*
vivaswathe:	=	to *vivaswa:n* (the Sun);
vivaswa:n	=	the Sun
pra:ha	=	taught (this)
manave:	=	to Manu;
manuhu	=	the Manu
abravi:th	=	taught (this)
ikshwa:kave:	=	to Ikshwa:ku

Purport

The Lord clarifies that this karma yo:ga is not something that He is making up to motivate Arjuna to wage this war. For liberation of all from the cycle of birth and death, He initiated Vivaswa:n into this (imperishable) eternal yo:ga at the beginning of this manvanthara. Then Vivasw:an (the Sun) initiated his son, Manu Vaivaswatha into this yo:ga.

Note

1. The Sun is called Vivaswa:n because he illuminates everything with his radiance. The son of Vivaswa:n is called Vaivaswatha.
2. A manvanthara is period for which a Manu rules.
3. manvanthara = 71 de:va yugas =306,720,000 human years!!!!
4. This karma yo:ga is more than two billion years old. That is why the Lord refers to this yo:ga as avyayam.
5. The Sun came at the beginning of the present Kalpa(creation).
6. 1 kalpa   = 14 manvantharas =Total life span of our current Universe.
               = 14 X 71 de:va yugas
               = 14 X 71 X 12000 de:va years
               = 14 X 71 X 12000 X 360 human years
               = 4,294,080,000 human years
7. We are in the 7th manvanthara. So, the Sun we see has been shining for 2.1 billion years! Our manu is Vaivaswatha, the son of the Sun.
8. Since this yo:ga started from Lord through Sun carried on until now and going to be there forever. Thus it is avyaya (eternal)

SLOKA-2

e:vam parampara: pra:ptham
imam ra:jarshayo: viduhu |
sa ka:le:ne:ha mahatha:
yo:go: nashtah paranthapa! || 2

Word Split

e:vam – parampara: pra:ptham
imam – ra:jarshayaha – viduhu |
saha – ka:le:na – iha – mahatha:
yo:gaha – nashtaha – paranthapa! ||

Meaning

paranthapa!	=	Oh! Arjuna! (
imam	=	this science of *karma yo:ga*
parampara: pra:ptham	=	is passed on through generations
e:vam	=	in this manner.
ra:jarshayaha	=	The saintly kings
viduhu	=	understood this.
saha	=	That knowledge
yo:gaha	=	of *karma yo:ga*
iha	=	in this world
nashtaha	=	was lost
mahatha:	=	over a long duration of
ka:le:na	=	time.

Purport

The Lord explains why this important *yo:ga* was lost. He had taught this yo:ga more than two billion years ago. The sages transmitted this from one generation to the next generation till now. However, not all recipients were the brightest of students. Thus, because of the long lapse of time and the differences in the receptive powers of those who got this yo:ga, this yo:ga has disappeared from the world. There were some Kings like Janaka and Ambari:sha who knew it in the past. Bhi:shma, Vya:sa, and Akru:ra (from Arjuna's time) know it still, but such people are very rare.

Note

1. Royal sages are kings who have a wisdom and generosity of Rushies. Krushna took examples of Rajarshies to show Arjuna that Kings, while being Jna:nies still followed karmayo:ga and did their duty and fought war as a part of their dharma.
2. Arjuna is called paranthapa, means one who can frighten enemies with his valor.
3. The Lord said that karma yo:ga as avyaya in the first sloka and mahatha: ka:le:na nashtaha in second slo:ka. If it disappeared, then how can we call it avyaya? Our purva:cha:ryas answered this question in their commentaries. Over a long period of time, the number of people practicing karma yo:ga became less and less. Thus it is said as nashtaha, which does not mean the complete loss. There are a few people like Vya:sa and Ambari:sha etc who practiced this yo:ga, so it has not disappeared completely.
4. The Lord taught karma yo:ga to the Sun in the beginning of this universe. He is now teaching the same to Arjuna in the form of Krushna. As the Lord is eternal, the knowledge blessed by Him is also eternal are sa:swatha i.e. avyaya.
5. As karma yo:ga will be continued in the future generations also, we can call it as sa:swatha/ avyaya.

SLOKA-3

sa e:va:yam maya: the::dya
yo:gah pro:kthah pura:thanaha |
bhaktho::si me: sakha: che:thi
rahasyam hye:thad uththamam || 3

Word Split

saha – e:va – ayam – maya: – the: – adya
yo:gaha – pro:kthaha – pura:thanaha
bhakthaha – asi – me: – sakha: – cha– ithi
rahasyam – hi – e:thath – uththamam

Meaning

ayam	=	This
pura:thanaha	=	ancient and evergreen
yo:gaha	=	karma yo:ga
saha e:va	=	is the same one (revealed to the Sun)
uththamam	=	and is a precious
rahasyam hi	=	secret;
adya	=	today,

e:thath	=	this
pro:kthaha	=	is revealed (taught)
the:	=	to you
maya:	=	by Me
asi	=	(because) you are
bhakthaha	=	My devotee
cha	=	and
sakha:	=	My friend.

Purport

Unless something is practiced intelligently, it will not survive in all its glory for long. The karma yo:ga has all but disappeared because not many were able to practice it. The previous verse gave reasons for the decline of the practice of this yo:ga.

This karma yo:ga is crucial for the well-being of oneself and society, so it is important to revive its practice. The practice is purposeful when the reasoning behind it is clear. Otherwise, it will remain mechanical and could degenerate into mere superstition.

Thus, karma yo:ga is worth preserving and practicing for the liberation of indivuals and also for social welfare. In the past, the Lord Himself revealed this for the benefit of all. Great royal sages, generous and gifted intellectuals practiced it, becoming role-models for others. This is a venerable tradition that must be kept alive. For all these and more reasons, the Lord compassionately is ready to expound on this karma yo:ga further.

Note

Only the omniscient and compassionate Lord can bring the necessary clarity to karma yo:ga now for four main reasons:
1. Arjuna sought this knowledge from Him.
2. He is available to give that knowledge now
3. He is the One Who taught it well to Sun more than two billion years ago!
4. No one except Lord knows all aspects of this karma yo:ga perfectly, so He alone is the best source of this knowledge.

SLOKA-4

arjuna uva:cha

avaram bhavatho: janma
param janma vivaswathaha |
kattham e:thad vija:ni:ya:m
thwam a:dau pro:kthava:n ithi || 4

Word Split

arjunaha – uva:cha

avaram – bhavathaha – janma
param– janma – vivaswathaha
kattham – e:thath – vija:ni:ya:m
thwam – a:dau – pro:kthava:n – ithi

Meaning

arjuna	=	Arjuna
uva:cha	=	said
bhavathaha	=	your
janma	=	birth
aparam	=	is recent;
vivaswathaha	=	the sun's
janma	=	birth
param	=	is ancient;
kattham	=	how
vija:ni:ya:m	=	(shall i) understand
ithi	=	that
thwam	=	you
pro:kthva:n	=	taught (initiated)
e:thath	=	(Sun into) this
a:dau	=	in the beginning?

Purport

Arjuna heard of the divinity of the Lord from various sources like Bhi:shma, Vya:sa, and many sages that he met during his exile. He saw the Lord come to their aid in many mysterious ways by saving Draupadi in the royal court, by turning back Du:rva:sa who had come at an inopportune time, and so on.

Now, when the Lord Himself declares His transcendence, by revealing that He taught Vivaswa:n billions of years ago, Arjuna could not control his curiosity and asked a loaded question.

There are six questions embedded in this single question. We infer this based on the answers the Lord gives in the next few verses. (uththara:th prasna unne:yaha)

1. Like ours, are your births also real too?
2. If so, are Your powers of omniscience, omnipotence, lordship etc with You?
3. Like ours, is Your body made up of the five elements?
4. Like ours, is Your birth due to *karma* too or due to your wish and will?
5. Like us, are You born when the *karma* ripens? (parithra:na:ya)
6. Like us, are You born to experience the duality of pain and pleasure?

SLOKA-5

sri: bhagava:n uva:cha

bahu:ni me: vyathi:tha:ni
janma:ni thava cha:rjuna ! |
tha:nyaham ve:da sarva:ni
na thwam ve:tthha paramthapa! || 5

Word Split

sri: bhagava:n - uva:cha

bahu:ni – me: – vyathi:tha:ni
janma:ni – thava– cha– arjuna |
tha:ni – aham– ve:da – sarva:ni
na – thwam – ve:tthha – paramthapa ||

Meaning

sri: bhagavan	=	*The Lord*
uva:cha	=	*said*
arjuna	=	O Arjuna!
bahu:ni	=	many
janma:ni	=	births
me:	=	of mine
cha	=	and also
thava	=	of yours
vyathi:tha:ni	=	have passed;
paranthapa!	=	O scorcher of the enemies!
aham	=	I
ve:da	=	know
sarva:ni	=	all
tha:ni	=	those
thwam	=	(but) you
na	=	(do) not
ve:ttha	=	know

Purport

    The Lord says "I had many births, and so did you. I know them all, but you do not"

The Lord reveals the secret of His divine births:

1. to cleanse sinful thoughts from our hearts
2. to help us listen to Him attentively.

    The Lord answers the first implied question of Arjuna. The Lord affirms that His births are not illusory. They are as real as Arjuna's and ours. We don't remember about our previous births because of our ka:rmic bondage. The Lord does not forget because He does not have ka:rmic bondage.

Note

    How did Lord's reply to the first implied question established that His births are "real" and

not "illusory"? Lord used two words to establish the real nature of His birth: bahu:ni, vyathi:tha:ni.

In illusion there is no concept of single or many. Similarly, there is no concept of timeline either. By using these two words he established that His births and our births are real and not an illusion.

For example, when a magician takes a pigeon out of his hat, it is an illusion because, the pigeon is not taking birth at that moment. It is not dying when he puts it back in the hat. In this illusory magic trick there is no birth and death of the pigeon. Ours and Lords births in this universe are different from this magic trick. They are real.

SLOKA-6

ajo::pi sannavyaya:thma:
bhu:tha:na:m i:swaro::pisan |
prakruthim swa:m adhishtta:ya
sambhava:my a:thma ma:yaya: || 6

Word Split
ajaha – api – san – avyaya:thma:
bhu:tha:na:m – i:swaraha – api – san |
prakruthim – swa:m – adhishtta:ya
sambhava:mi – a:thma ma:yaya:

Meaning
api san	=	Though
ajaha	=	unborn,
api san	=	though
avyaya:thma:	=	changeless,
api san	=	though
i:swaraha	=	the lord
bhu:tha:na:m	=	of all those who are born,
sambhava:mi	=	I take birth
a:thma ma:yaya:	=	by my own wish (sankalpa),
adhishtta:ya	=	controlling
swa:m	=	my
prakruthim	=	transcendental nature

Purport
The Lord answers Arjuna's 2nd, 3rd and 4th questions in this verse.

The Lord takes birth without losing His inherent nature. All His infinite auspicious qualities and powers are intact even in His vibhava forms. He specifically mentions three of His auspicious qualities - *ajathwam, avyayathwam, and i:swarathwam*. He is *aja* because He doesn't have ka:rmic bondage. He is *avyaya:thama:* because he never falls from His nature. He is i:swaraha because He is the Lord, governing all.

The Lord's body is made up of five upanishaths, while our births are governed by karma and our bodies are made up of the five elements of this nature. This is the answer to Arjuna's third question.

The Lord's *sankalpa* is the reason for His births. He can chose the time, place, and form for His descent, while we are subject to our karma and cannot chose when and how we are born. This is the answer to Arjuna's fourth question.

SLOKA-7

yada: yada: hi dharmasya
gla:nir bhavathi bha:ratha! |
abhyuttha:nam adharmasya
thada:thma:nam sruja:myaham || 7

Word Split

yada: – yada: – hi – dharmasya
gla:nihi – bhavathi – bha:ratha!
Abhyuttha:nam – adharmasya
thada: – a:thma:nam – sruja:mi – aham

Meaning

bha:ratha	=	O descendant of Bharatha (Arjuna)!
yada: yada: hi	=	Whenever
gla:nihi	=	deterioration
bhavathi	=	happens
dharmasya	=	to dharma
abhyuttha:nam	=	(and) dominance
bhavathi	=	happens
adharmasya	=	to adharma,
thada:	=	then
aham	=	I
sruja:mi	=	manifest
a:thma:nam	=	Myself.

Purport

The Lord answers Arjuna's 5th question here. He wanted to know when the Lord takes birth. While we take births whenever our *karma* dictates, the Lord takes birth whenever *dharma* declines, and He makes sure that *dharma* flourishes again.

We should remember that *dharma* is a means authorized by the *Ve:da*s to accomplish our goals. These means are beneficial to all in every society. There are many means to accommodate differences in aptitude and experiences of diverse beings. They regulate life so that all can exist harmoniously. *A:cha:ryas* and other role models like Janaka follow *dharma* to set us an example. However, some rebel against *dharma* and corrupt others. They make life difficult, especially to those who follow dharma. They become so powerful that nobody can win against them. It is at this time that the Lord intervenes by taking births as needed to restrain evil.

SLOKA-8

parithra:**na**:ya sa:dhu:na:m
vina:**sa**:ya cha dushkrutha:m |
dharma samsttha:pana:rttha:ya
sambhava:mi yuge: yuge: || 8

Word Split

parithra:**na**:ya – sa:dhu:na:m
vina:**sa**:ya – cha – dushkrutha:m |
dharma samsttha:pana:rttha:ya
sambhava:mi – yuge: yuge: ||

Meaning

sambhava:mi	=	I manifest
yuge: yuge:	=	in every era
parithra:**na**:ya	=	for the protection
sa:dhu:na:m	=	of good people,
vina:**sa**:ya	=	for the complete destruction
dushkrutha:m	=	of evil doers
cha	=	and also
arttha:ya	=	for
dharma-samsttha:pana	=	the firm establishment of dharma

Purport

The Lord answers Arjuna's last question here. The Lord is not affected by duality of pleasure and pain like us. Nevertheless, the Lord does not like to see *sa:dhus* or the good people come to any harm. He will do whatever is needed to protect them.

Who are *sa:dhus*? They are people who do everything as a prayerful offering to the Lord. They live for the Lord. His *li:las* and *kalya:na gunas* are their lifeline. They are ever-immersed in thinking about and relishing His manifestations and His deeds during those manifestations. Devotees like Prahla:da and the a:lwa:rs are examples of *sa:dhus*.

Since the Lord is here in our world to please the *sa:dhus*, He also removes all evil-doers who hurts *sa:dhus* and dharma. Thus, He establishes dharma and reforms the society.

Sloka-9

janma karma cha me: divyam
e:vam yo: ve:ththi thaththwathaha |
thyakthwa: de:ham punarjanma
naithi ma:m e:thi so::rjuna! || 9

Word Split

janma – karma – cha – me: – divyam
e:vam – yaha – ve:ththi – thaththwathaha
thyakthwa: – de:ham – punarjanma
na – e:thi – ma:m – e:thi – saha – arjuna!

Meaning

arjuna	=	O Arjuna!
yaha	=	Whoever
ve:ththi	=	knows
thaththwathaha	=	in reality
e:vam	=	that
me:	=	My
janma	=	birth
cha	=	and
karma	=	actions
divyam	=	are divine,
saha	=	that person
na+ e:thi	=	never gets
punaha + janma	=	another birth
thyakthawa:	=	(and) after leaving
de:ham	=	the present body
e:thi	=	attains
ma:m	=	Me.

Purport

There are two things that we must keep in mind about the divinity of the Lord's manifestations:

1. The Lord is omniscient and omnipotent. His birth is according to His *sankalpa* and from His *prakruthi*. Thus, His *janma* is divine.

2. The Lord is not bound to *karma* by anyone or anything. It is because of His absolute grace and compassion that He does *karma* for the enlightenment of all *ji:vas*. Thus, His *karma* is divine.

The Lord reveals the secrets of His divine *janma* and *karma* that are crucial to attain Him. Knowing these two secrets increases our love for Him and our desire to serve Him. This libertes us from ka:rmic bondage. The Lord elaborates further in the coming verses.

SLOKA-10

vi:tha ra:ga bha:yakro:dha:ha
manmaya: ma:m upa:sritha:ha |
bahavo: jna:na thapasa:
pu:tha: madbha:vam a:gatha:ha || 10

Word Split

vi:tha ra:ga bha:yakro:dha:ha

manmaya:ha – ma:m – upa:sritha:ha

bahavaha – jna:na thapasa:

pu:tha:ha – madbha:vam – a:gatha:ha

Meaning

pu:tha:ha	=	Purified
jna:na thapasa:	=	by the knowledge of His manifestations, which is a penance in itself,

vi:tha ra:ga bhaya kro:dha:ha

vi:tha	=	freed from
ra:ga	=	attachment
bhaya	=	fear
kro:dha:ha	=	(and) anger,
manmaya:ha	=	fully absorbed in Me,
upa:sritha:ha	=	(and) taking refuge
ma:m	=	in Me,
bahavaha	=	many
a:gatha:ha	=	attained
madbha:vam	=	a state similar to Mine (sa:dharmyam).

Purport

Knowing about the divinity of the Lord's *janma* and *karma* is a means of purification. This knowledge is called *avatha:ra rahasya jna:nam* or the secret of His manifestations. It is a means for liberation. In this verse, He explains how this knowledge gets rid of our ka:rmic bondage.

Knowing about the Lord's supremacy and transcendence and His compassion and benevolence increases our respect and love for Him. As a result, we spend more and more of our thought on Him, His deeds and His qualities. This is *thapas*. Our purity goes up. Simultaneously, we spend less and less of our thoughts on sinful things. This results in reduction of *ra:ga, kro:dha and bhaya*. Our sins go down. When sins no longer distract us, we can surrender to the Lord, holding Him very dear to us. As a result, we can easily fix our thought on the Lord and get to a state that is similar to the Lord's.

Note

1. When we are attached to something for our sense-gratification, it is called ra:ga.

2. The thought of losing that sense-gratification or the thought of facing unwanted things is called bhaya or fear.

3. The thought of taking revenge when someone obstructs our gratification is called anger or kro:dha.

4. Sa:dharmyam means getting qualities similar to the Lord's.

SLOKA-11

ye: yattha: ma:m prapadyanthe:
tha:ms thatthaiva bhaja:my aham |
mama varthma: nuvarthanthe:
manushya:h pa:rttha! sarvasaha || 11

Word Split

ye: – yattha: – ma:m– prapadyanthe:
tha:n – thattha: – e:va– bhaja:mi – aham |
mama – varthma – anuvarthanthe:
manushya:ha – pa:rttha! – sarvasaha ||

Meaning

pa:rttha!	=	O Son of Pruttha (Arjuna)!
ye:	=	Those who
prapadyanthe:	=	worship
ma:m	=	me
yattha:	=	in whatever way they like,
thattha:+ e:va	=	in the very same way
aham	=	I
bhaja:mi	=	reciprocate
tha:n	=	to them;
manushya:ha	=	men
anuvarthanthe:	=	experience
mama	=	my
varthma	=	divine nature
sarvasaha	=	in all their preferred forms.

Purport

    In the earlier verses, the Lord revealed about His manifestations—the purpose, occasion and so on. We might feel bad that we missed the opportunity of seeing, hearing, touching, and associating with the Lord. We might wonder if there is any way that we too can be with the Lord.

    We are with the Lord all the time, but we might not be aware of it. The Lord is inside and outside all. The *antharya:mi* or the indweller in all beings, is invisible to our eyes. The *vibhava* or the Manifestation is time-bound. He comes, accomplishes His task, and goes away. The *vyu:ha* or the Reclining form on A:dise:sha in the Milk-Ocean, is beyond our physical reach, not to mention the *para* or the Transcendental Form. We seem to be out of luck.

    To comfort us, the Lord says that He is accessible to anyone who really wants to associate with Him. For those who want to see and touch Him, He blesses them by becoming *archa:* or the Deity form of their choice. For those who love Him as their lord or parent or brother or friend or child or husband etc., He reciprocates their love in the same way. After all, He is the Supreme and Independent, and thus can choose to be compassionate in any way He and the devotee wants.

SLOKA-12

ka:nkshanthah karma**n**a:m siddhim
yajantha iha de:vatha:ha |
kshipram hi ma:nushe: lo:ke:
siddhir bhavathi karmaja: || 12

Word Split

ka:nkshanthaha – karma**n**a:m – siddhim

yajanthaha – iha – de:vatha:ha

kshipram – hi – ma:nushe: lo:ke:

siddhihi – bhavathi – karmaja:

Meaning

ka:nkshanthaha	=	expecting
siddhim	=	rewards
karma**n**a:m	=	for doing *karma*,
iha	=	people in this world
yajanthaha	=	worship
de:vatha:ha	=	de:vathas
hi	=	because
ma:nushe: lo:ke:	=	in this world of men
siddhihi	=	rewards (like getting kids, animals, spouse etc.)
karmaja:	=	resulting from karma
bhavathi	=	occur
kshipram	=	quickly.

Purport

The Supreme Lord is compassionate, accessible, and competent to grant our prayers, yet not all approach Him. In this verse, He lets us know why that is the case.

Many look for instant gratification. We choose to take a penny today rather than a dollar tomorrow. If we can help it, we would rather bag rewards even before the activity is performed. That is how impatient and juvenile we are in our approach to life. As a result, we choose to do rites dedicated to *de:vatha*s that promise instant results. Our past *samska:ra*s blind us to the knowledge that the Lord too can bestow those results and much more beyond that. We do not choose to perform *karma yo:ga*. Consequently, we find it hard to get out of this vicious cycle.

SLOKA-13

cha:thur varnyam maya: srushtam
guna karma vibha:gasaha|
thasya kartha:ram api ma:m
viddhyakartha:ram avyayam || 13

Word Split

cha:thurvarnyam – maya: – srushtam
guna karma vibha:gasaha -
thasya – kartha:ram – api – ma:m
viddhi – akartha:ram – avyayam

Meaning

cha:thurvarnyam	=	the four divisions (of all beings)
srushtam	=	were created
maya:	=	by Me
guna karma vibha:gasaha	=	based on (their) *guna* and *karma;*
viddhi	=	know
ma:m	=	Me,
avyayam	=	the unchangeable,
akartha:ram	=	as the *akartha: (non-doer)* for the division
api	=	even though
kartha:ram	=	am the *kartha:* (the doer)
thasya	=	of the division.

Purport

The Lord has created all the beings in this universe, divided into four var**n**as or divisions:

1. *de:va* or the de:vathas
2. *ma:nushya* or the human beings
3. *thiryak* or the other moving living beings (like, birds, animals, insects etc.)
4. *sttha:vara* or the non-moving beings (like, trees, rocks etc.)

In these mutually exclusive and collectively exhaustive categories, are included all manifested worlds. These var**n**as are based on *karma* and *guna*. In other words, whatever *janma* we get is to work out the *karma* based on the predominant *gunas* of our previous lives. Thus, we have to engage in *karma* assigned to us based on our *gunas* in previous lives. If we do this *karma* as His worship, it liberates us. However, if we do this *karma* for our sense-gratification, then it binds us further in this *karmic bondage.*

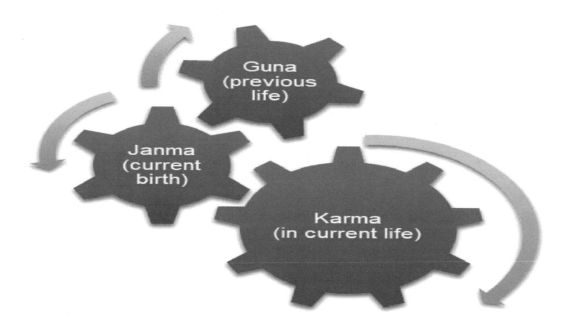

Thus, we have to congratulate or blame only ourselves for our birth and our experiences in this world, not the Lord. We must realize that He never undergoes any change. He is not responsible for our varna and its consequences. He impartially facilitates our experiencing of the ka:rmic actions that we have piled up. As humans, we practice karma yo:ga based on our varna which is the result of our guna and karma.

SLOKA-14

na ma:m karma:**ni** limpanthi
na me: karmaphale: spruha: |
ithi ma:m yo::bhija:na:thi
karmabhir na sa baddhyathe: || 14

Word Split

na – ma:m – karma:**ni** – limpanthi
na – me: – karmaphale: – spruha:
ithi – ma:m – yaha – abhija:na:thi
karmabhihi – na – saha – baddhyathe:

Meaning

karma:**ni**	=	The activities I do, like creation etc.
na limpanthi	=	do not stain
ma:m	=	Me;
me:	=	I have
na spruha:	=	(there is) no interest
karmaphale:	=	in the rewards for those activities;
ithi	=	thus
saha	=	he
yaha	=	who
abhija:na:thi	=	knows
ma:m	=	Me
na	=	is not
baddhyathe:	=	bound
karmabhihi	=	by *karma* (that he does).

Purport

The Lord is untouched (not bound) by the activities of creating the worlds, sustaining them or withdrawing them. However, we are bound by our *karma*. Why? The Lord answers this question and highlights for us the way out of ka:rmic bondage.

The Lord has no *karmaphala:sakthi*. He compassionately and competently creates worlds etc. so that *ji:vas* can work out their *karma* and uplift themselves. He does these for our sake, not His own.

We, on the other hand, work because we want to gratify ourselves. We think, "I am doing this with my resources so that I can enjoy the reward." This *karthruthwam* (I am doing) and *sangam* (with my resources) lead to *karmaphala:sakthi* (for my enjoyment of the reward). This *karmaphala:sakthi* strengthens our ka:rmic bondage. That is why the Lord has no ka:rmic bondage, but we do. When we understand this, we too can find a way to get out of ka:rmic bondage.

SLOKA-15

e:vam jna:thwa: krutham karma
pu:rvair api mumukshubhihi |
kuru karmaiva thasma:th thwam
pu:rvaih pu:rvatharam krutham || 15

Word Split

e:vam – jna:thwa: – krutham – karma
pu:rvaihi – api – mumukshubhihi
kuru – karma – e:va – thasma:th – thwam
pu:rvaihi – pu:rvatharam – krutham

Meaning

e:vam	=	Thus
jna:thwa:	=	knowing the secrets of my incarnations
karma	=	*karma yo:ga*
krutham	=	was practiced;
mumukshubhihi api	=	even by the *mumukshu*s (seekers of liberation)
pu:rvaihi	=	of olden times
thasma:th	=	therefore,
thwam (api)	=	you (also)
kuru	=	do
e:va	=	just
pu:rvatharam	=	the age old
karma	=	*karma yo:ga*
krutham	=	as done
pu:rvaihi	=	by those of the olden times.

Purport

    The great ones perform *karma* without *karthruthwam, sangam, and karmaphala:sakthi*. The ancients like the Sun, Manu, I:kshava:ku, Bhi:shma, Janaka, Ambari:sha, and many others have thus performed *karma yo:ga* (review Chapter 3). I revealed the *karma yo:ga* to the Sun. Thus it is older than the Sun. This time-tested, powerful karma yo:ga purified them. It will purify Arjuna when he engages in it. It will purify us too when we do it.

SLOKA-16

kim karma kim akarme:thi
kavayo::py athra mo:hitha:ha |
thath the: karma pravakshya:mi
yad jna:thwa: mo:kshyase::subha:th || 16

Word Split

kim – karma – kim – akarma – ithi
kavayaha – api – athra – mo:hitha:ha |
thath – the: – karma – pravakshya:mi
yath – jna:thwa: – mo:kshyase: – asubha:th

Meaning

kim	=	What is
karma	=	the *karma* practiced by *mumukshu*s?
kim	=	what is
akarma	=	the hidden *a:thmajna:na* (knowledge of the true self?)
api	=	even
kavayaha	=	the wise
mohitha:ha	=	are perplexed
ithi athra	=	about these;
pravakshya:mi	=	I shall clarify
the:	=	to you
thath	=	that
karma	=	*karma* as my worship (*karmayo:ga*)
jna:thwa: yath	=	knowing which
mo:kshyase:	=	you will be liberated
asubha:th	=	from this evil (ka:rmic bondage).

Purport

What is the *karma* that leads to liberation? What is *akarma*, the true nature of the self or *a:thmajna:na* that is hidden in the *karma yo:ga*? The Lord points out that even the wise are perplexed about these. No wonder many of us do not know how *a:thamajna:na* is hidden in the *karma yo:ga*. Many *mumukshu*s (those who seek liberation) are not clear about which *karma* to do to get liberated. They do not know how to do it without getting entangled. The Lord says that He is going to elaborate on this further so that Arjuna and other aspirants can follow and get liberation from ka:rmic bondage.

SLOKA- 17

karma**n**o: hyapi bo:ddhavyam
bo:ddhavyam cha vikarma**n**aha |
akarma**n**as cha bo:ddhavyam
gahana: karma**n**o: gathihi || 17

Word Split

karma**n**aha – hi – api – bo:ddhavyam
bo:ddhavyam – cha – vikarma**n**aha |
akarma**n**aha – cha – bo:ddhavyam
gahana: – karma**n**aha – gathihi

Meaning

karma**n**aha api	=	About *karma*
bo:ddhavyam	=	should be known,
vikarma**n**aha cha	=	and about *vikarma*, different kinds of *karma*
bo:dhavyam	=	should be known,
akarma**n**aha + cha	=	and about *akarma* that is the knowledge of *a:thma*
bo:ddhavyam	=	should be known
hi	=	because
gathihi	=	the way
karma**n**aha	=	of *karma*
gahana:	=	is unfathomable.

Purport

    It is worth knowing further about *karma* since it has to be performed in a proper way as the means for liberation. It is also important to know about *akarma*, real nature of *a:thma*, since it reveals the hidden *jna:na* in the *karma yo:ga*. It is also crucial to know about *vikarma*. We will understand how to perform *karma* properly only when we have a good understanding of these various aspects of karma.

Note

1. There are three kinds of vikarmas (diverse actions):

    a. Nithya (regular everyday duties like brushing, bathing, studying scriptures)

    b. Naimiththika (periodic duties like celebrating festivals, birthdays)

    c. Ka:mya (optional karma done to fulfill one's desires).

2. This vikarma is of various kinds because there are differences in the means of livelihood and the ways the livelihood is earned. What should be understood about vikarma is that even if it is diverse, the end result is the same — liberation from ka:rmic bondage — if done as a prayerful offering to the Lord.

SLOKA-18

karma**n**y akarma yah pa**s**ye:th
akarma**n**i cha karma yaha |
sa buddhima:n manushye:shu
sa yukthah kruthsna karmakruth || 18

Word Split

karma**n**i — akarma — yaha — pa**s**ye:th
akarma**n**i — cha — karma — yaha
saha — buddhima:n — manushye:shu
saha — yukthaha — kruthsna karmakruth

Meaning

saha	=	He
yaha	=	who
pa**s**ye:th	=	perceives
akarma	=	the true nature of *a:thma*
karma**n**i	=	in *karma* (while performing activities),
cha	=	and
yaha	=	who
pa**s**ye:th	=	perceives
karma	=	*karma* (action)
akarma**n**i	=	in the true nature of *a:thma*
buddhima:n	=	is intelligent
manushye:shu	=	among men;
saha	=	he
karmakruth	=	has completed
kruththsna	=	all *karma*
yukthaha	=	(and thus) is eligible for liberation from ka:rmic bondage.

Purport

The Lord says that:
1. We should perceive akarma (the true nature of the soul—a:thmajna:nam) in karma.
2. We should perceive karma in akarma.

Only when are able to do the two above, we can overcome ka:rmic bondage.

Perceiving *akarma* in *karma* – We must continually engage ourselves in *karma*. While doing so, we must not do it mechanically. We must be aware of how and why and when and where *karma* should be done. Only when thus competently done is the *karma* a useful means for liberation from ka:rmic bondage.

For example — learning to play the flute is *karma*. We learn about the flute, how to hold it, how to blow into it, and so on. This is *akarma*, the knowledge part of playing the flute. It guides our practice. It makes us recognize and correct our mistake so that we become proficient in playing the flute. Thus, *karma* here is practicing to play the flute, and *akarma* here is knowing how to practice appropriately. This is how we perceive *akarma* in *karma*.

Perceiving *karma* in *akarma* — We must know that even we are not physically engaged in *karma* but are meditating on the nature of the soul, there is the action of meditat**ing**. Here, *karma* is making the *yo:gi* to be in *akarma* by meditating, by understanding the true nature of the soul, by getting *a:thmajna:na* and so on.

For example, we know how to play the flute. Now, this knowledge remains knowledge if we don't actually play the flute. When we play the flute at a concert, we are letting *karma* of giving a public performance bring out that *akarma* or knowledge of playing the flute in public in a useful way. Thus, *karma* here is the playing of the flute, and *akarma* is the complete knowledge of how to play the flute. This is how we perceive *karma* in a*karma*.

Thus when we understand the interrelationship between knowledge and action or *akarma* and *karma* properly, we will not 'give up' *karma* but do it intelligently. Knowing the Lord's *avatha:ra rahasyam*, we competently engage in *karma* as a prayerful offering to Him. Such *karma* combined with knowledge becomes a means of liberation from our ka:rmic bondage.

Note
Remember that we can never really give up karma though some may think that they can. Those who think so are mu:ddhas or fools. Review Chapter 3 to recall this.

SLOKA-19

yasya sarve: sama:rambha:ha
ka:masankalpa varjitha:ha |
jna:na:gni dagdha karma:**n**am
tham a:huh pa**nd**itham budha:ha || 19

Word Split
yasya — sarve: — sama:rambha:ha
ka:masankalpa varjitha:ha
jna:na:gni dagdha karma:**n**am
tham — a:huhu — pa**nd**itham — budha:ha

Meaning
budha:ha	=	The enlightened
a:huhu	=	call
tham	=	that one
pa**nd**itham	=	the wise
yasya	=	whose
sama:rambha:ha	=	*karmas*
sarve:	=	are all
varjitha:ha	=	devoid of
ka:ma	=	the desire for rewards
sankalpa	=	(and) the misconceiving of the body as the soul
karma:**n**am	=	(and) whose *karma*

daghdha	=	is burnt up
jna:na:gni	=	by the fire of *a:thmajna:na*.

Purport

Any *karma* that is in progress is called *sama:rambha*. In this verse, *sankalpa* means identifying the body as the soul. It is a misconception and is called as *de:ha:thma bhra:nthi*. This makes us think that anything that is being done by the body is being done by us, the *ji:va*. As a result, we claim the results emanating from the *karma* as ours. This is *ka:ma*. This strengthens ka:rmic bondage.

Those who have no illusion that the body is the soul and have no *karmaphala:sakthi* are recognized as the wise by the enlightened. The wise know that *karma* is done by the body, so they do not hanker after rewards of *karma*. Thus, this fire of wisdom, *jna:na:gni*, burns up all their accumulated karma and releases them from the dreadful ka:rmic bondage.

SLOKA- 20

thyakthwa: karma phala:sangam
nithyathruptho: nira:**s**rayaha |
karma**n**y abhi pravruththo:pi
naiva kimchith karo:thi saha || 20

Word Split

thyakthwa: — karma phala:sangam
nithyathrupthaha — nira:**s**rayaha
karma**ni** — abhi pravruththaha — api
na — e:va — kimchith — karo:thi — saha

Meaning

nithya thrupthaha	=	Fulfilled with the eternal *a:thma*,
nira:**s**rayaha	=	not subject to nature,
thyakthwa:	=	having given up
karmaphala:sangam	=	attachment to rewards,
api abhi pravruththaha	=	though fully engaged
karma**ni**	=	in *karma*,
saha	=	he
e:va	=	certainly
na	=	does not
karo:thi	=	do
kinchith	=	anything.

Purport

The wise one is *nithya thruptha* or fulfilled since he intuits the ever blissful eternal *a:thma*. Though outwardly he interacts with nature, he inwardly knows that nothing in the ever changing nature is a reliable or steady support. Thus, he has no *karma phala:sakthi* and no attraction for anything in nature. Despite that, he continually engages in *karma* without getting bound by it. His *karma* has been transformed by *a:thma jna:na.* As a result he is no longer considered to be a doer of *karma* even when he does.

SLOKA- 21

nira:**si**:r yatha chiththa:thma:
thyaktha sarvwa parigrahaha |
sa:ri:ram ke:valam karma
kurvann a:pno:thi kilbisham || 21

Word Split

nira:**si**:hi — yatha chiththa:thma:
thyaktha sarwa parigrahaha
sa:ri:ram — ke:valam — karma
kurvan — na — a:pno:thi — kilbisham

Meaning

nira:**si**:hi	=	without hankering for rewards
yatha chiththa:thma:	=	having controlled mind and intelligence,
thyaktha sarwa parigrahaha	=	having given up possessiveness completely,
(saha)	=	he
karma kurvan	=	does karma
sa:ri:ram ke:valam	=	that can be done with the body alone
na + a:pno:thi	=	(but) never gets
kilbisham	=	sinful ka:rmic bondage.

Purport

When the mind does not hanker after sense gratification, it does not seek rewards for *karma*. It does not jump from one thought to another restlessly in pursuit of objects in nature. It, therefore, becomes serene. With such a mind, the wise man continues to work effectively with his body. He remains untouched by sin.

SLOKA- 22

yadruchha: la:bha santhushto:
dwandwa:thi:tho: vimathsaraha |
samas siddha:va siddhau cha
kruthwa::pi na nibaddhyathe: || 22

Word Split

yadruchha: la:bha santhushtaha
dwandwa:thi:thaha — vimathsaraha
samaha — siddhau — siddhau — cha
kruthwa — api — na — nibaddhyathe:

Meaning

(saha)	=	He who is
santhushto:	=	content
yadruchha: la:bha	=	with whatever he comes across,
dwandwa:thi:thaha	=	beyond duality (of heat/cold, pain/pleasure etc.),
vimathsaraha	=	free from ill-will,
samaha	=	(and) balanced
siddhau	=	in success
asiddhau cha	=	and in failure
na nibhadyathe:	=	does not get bound
kruthwa: api	=	even when engaged in *karma*.

Purport

In this verse, the Lord essentially gives us 4 more qualities that we should cultivate so that we don't get bound by our *karma*:

1. contentment in the material world
2. freedom from dualities
3. freedom from ill-will
4. balance when facing ups and downs while doing *karma*

The mumukshu does not insist on a particular kind of food or clothing or shelter. He is fine with whatever works because his focus is not on enjoying the food, clothing, or shelter. His eyes are set on the goal of a:thmajna:na. As a result, he gives up anything that comes in the way of the goal. If they cannot be given up, he puts up with them patiently. He does not get irritated or thrilled with others or with results. He does not impose karthruthwam on himself or on others, so he does not hold himself or others responsible for the results of karma. Moreover, he does not consider the worldly dealings to be more important than his goal. Pain or pleasure, love or hate, victory or defeat do not bother him. They don't make him think ill of anyone. In other words, the worldly people with their affairs cannot distract him from his goal. Undistracted, he serenely marches on towards his goal.

SLOKA- 23

gathasangasya mukthasya
jna:na:vastthitha che:thasaha |
yajna: ya:charathah karma
samagram pravili:yathe: || 23

Word Split

gathasangasya — mukthasya
jna:na:vastthitha che:thasaha
yajna:ya — a:charathaha— karma
samagram — pravili:yathe:

Meaning

(thasya)	=	His
samagram	=	complete
karma	=	ka:rmic stock
pravili:yathe:	=	gets wiped out
jna:na:vastthitha che:thasaha	=	whose mind is established in *a:thmajna:na*,
gathasangasya	=	who has no attachment for anything in nature,
mukthasya	=	who is liberated from worldly hankerings,
a:charathaha	=	(and) who works
yajna:ya	=	for the sake of *yajna*.

Purport

In the previous verse, the *mumukshu* had to put in effort to hold himself back from getting distracted by the powerful experiences of the world. In this verse, the Lord mentions the next stage of such an aspirant. Now, the *mumukshu*'s mind is already established in the *a:thma*. It spontaneously turns away from nature towards the bliss of *a:thma*. Finally, the accumulated previous *karma* that has been obstructing his *a:thmajna:na* is wiped out just as 'delete' function erases files on the computer.

At this stage, the mumukshu discharges his responsibilities well. He appropriately takes care of himself, his family, his society, his country, and his environment by doing all that he ought to. However, he does not get attached to them or the success of the projects he undertakes. He continues to perform *karma* as it should be done. His *karma* is now *yajna*. His work is worship.

In other words, the Lord gives 3 more qualities that we should keep in mind as we engage intelligently in *karma*:

1. we should remain in *a:thmajna:na*
2. we should not get distracted by anything or anyone else (*muktha sangaha*)
3. we should work as worship (*a:charathaha yajna:ya*).

SLOKA- 24

bramh:arpa**n**am bramhahavihi
bramha:gnau bramha**n**a: hutham |
bramhaiva the:na ganthavyam
bramha karma sama:dhina: || 24

Word Split

bramh:arpa**n**am — bramhahavihi
bramha:gnau — bramha**n**a: — hutham |
brahma — e:va — the:na — ganthavyam
bramha karma sama:dhina:

Meaning

the:na	=	By him who
bramha karma sama:dhina:	=	thinks of *bramha* to be the basis of all *karma*
bramha + eva	=	*bramha* alone
ganthavyam	=	will be attained
(because he will also have realized)		
havihi	=	the *ho:madravya*
brahma	=	as *bramha:thmaka*,
bramha:gnau	=	the *ho:ma:gni* as *bramha:thmaka*,
bramha:rpa**n**am	=	*sruk, sruva* through which offerings are made as *bramha:thmaka*,
bramha**n**a: hutham	=	the kartha: (by whom *ho:ma* is performed) as *brmha:thmaka*.

Purport

The mumukshu will come to a state in which he is conscious of the a:thma in everything he does or sees. He will perform ho:ma with a single-minded awareness of the a:thma that pervades inside the offering, the fire, the wooden spoons, and himself. Everything is pervaded by a:thma. The plurality of I/my or he/she/it or his/her/its or they/theirs etc. that we are aware of is not in this mumukshu at this stage. The mumukshu has completely spiritualized all his karma thus. Undoubtedly, he attains his goal of a:thmajna:na.

Note

1. bramha:thmika— Technically, it means, "having Bramhan as the a:thma." The Lord dwells inside and outside all and supports all. Whatever name anything or anyone has, is due to the Lord's indwelling presence that causes the existence of that thing or person. Therefore, anyone's name goes all the way to the Indwelling Lord. In that sense, the ho:ma supplies, the ho:ma doer, the ho:ma fire, and so on are all brahma:thmika.

2. ho:madravyas: they are offerings like rice, puro:da:sam, clarified butter/ghee in the ho:ma.

3. ho:ma:gni: it is the sacrificial fire has 3 different names. They are a:havaniya:gni, ga:rhapathya:gni , and dakshina:gni.

4. sruk and sruva: these are long handled wooden spoons used to pour offerings into the agni at the time of ya:jna.

SLOKA- 25

daivam e:va:pare: yajnam
yo:ginah paryupa:sathe: |
bramha:gna:vapare: yajnam
yajne: naivo:pa juhwathi || 25

Word Split

daivam — e:va — a:pare: — yajnam
yo:ginaha — paryupa:sathe: |
bramha:gnau — apare: — yajnam
yajne:na— e:va— upajuhwathi

Meaning

apare:	=	some
yo:ginaha	=	*karma yo:gi*s
paryupa:sathe:	=	perform the worship of
daivam	=	*de:vathas (archa* forms*)*
yajnam + e:va	=	as the only *yajna;*
apare:	=	some
upajuhva:thi	=	perform the *ho:ma*
yajne:na + eva	=	with the specific tools like *sruk sruva*
yajnam	=	and offerings
brahma+agnau	=	into *ho:ma:gni* (bramha in the form of agni)

Purport

From 25-29, the Lord reveals the secret of performing each karma as yajna

Some karma yo:gis are specially devoted to archa forms of de:vathas and worship them with great interest. They consider that worship itself as the yajna that they should perform. Yet other karma yo:gis are dedicated to the ho:mas or fire-sacrifices. They do them meticulously by following all the rules and regulations. They consider pouring the ho:madravayas into the ho:ma:gni as the yajna. All these yajnas are from the karmaka:nda portion of the Ve:das.

SLOKA- 26

sro:thra:di:n indriya:ny anye:
samyam a:gnishu juhwathi |
sabda:di:n vishaya:n anye:
indriya:gnishu juhwathi || 26

Word Split

sro:thra:di:n — indriya:ni — anye:
samyama:gnishu — juhwathi
sabda:di:n — vishaya:n — anye:
indriya:gnishu — juhwathi

Meaning

anye:	=	yet others
juhwathi	=	offer
indriya:**ni**	=	(their) senses
sro:thra:di:ni	=	like ears,
samyama+agnishu	=	into the fire of restraint;
anye:	=	some others
juhwathi	=	offer
vishya:n	=	the sense objects
sabda:di:n	=	like sound etc.
indriya:gnishu	=	into the fire of senses.

Purport

The Lord further mentions two other kinds of *karma yo:gi*s in this verse. He continues to use the analogy of *ho:ma*. He tells us what the *havis* or the offerings are to be poured into the fire *agni*.

Some of the *karma yo:gis* try to control their senses. They use their hearing etc. as *havis* to be poured into the fire of restraint. In other words, they try not to be distracted by hearing or seeing anything that is not related to their goal of *a:thmajna:na*. For example, when a team really wants to win the championship, they train very hard and don't get distracted by the cheers or jeers on the field.

Yet other *karma yo:gi*s use what they hear (sounds) etc. as *havis* to be poured into the fire of senses. In other words, they stay away from distractions. They hear only what they should. They see only what they should and so on. If anything inappropriate comes their way, they turn away from them. For example, when the team is training, each player knows he should eat the right kind of food to build the muscle needed to make big plays in the game. He does not go anywhere near ice-cream if that is forbidden for him during the training session.

Thus having disciplined senses is one form of *karmayo:ga*. Experiencing sensory objects as *yajna* is another form of *karmayo:ga*.

SLOKA- 27

sarva:**ni**:ndriya karma:**ni**
pra:**n**a karma:**ni** cha:pare: |
a:thma samyama yo:ga:gnau
juhwathi jna:na di:pithe: || 27

Word Split

sarva:**ni** — i:ndriya karma:**ni**
pra:**n**a karma:**ni** — cha — apare:
a:thma samyama yo:ga:gnau
juhwathi — jna:na di:pithe:

Meaning

apare:	=	Some others
jna:na di:pithe:	=	illumined by wisdom
juhwathi	=	offer

sarva:**ni**	=	all
indriyakarma:**ni**	=	functions of senses like seeing, hearing etc.
cha	=	and
pra:**na** karma:ni	=	functions of the pra:**na**
agnau	=	into the fire of
yo:ga	=	the practice
a:thma samyama	=	of mental discipline.

Purport

The *pra:na* gives energy to all the senses to function. The senses run after their objects in this ever-changing world. Knowing this, the *karma yo:gi* wisely controls them by disciplining his mind. He practices to control his mind by not getting attached to the world even as he engages in it with his *jna:ne:ndriyas* and *karme:ndriyas*. He offers the functions of *karme:ndriyas*, *jna:nendriyas* and the *pra:na* as *havis* into the fire of mental discipline.

Note

Pra:na while performing five activities is called as panchapra:na. They are 1) pra:na, 2) ap:na, 3) vya:na, 4) uda:na, 5) sama:na.

SLOKA- 28

dravya yajna:s thapo: yajna:ha
yo:gayajna:s thattha::pare: |
sva:dhya:ya jna:na yajna:s cha
yathayas samsritha vratha:ha || 28

Word Split

dravya yajna:ha — thapo: yajna:ha
yo:gayajna:ha — thattha: — apare:
swa:dhya:ya jna:na yajna:ha — cha
yathayaha — samsritha vratha:ha

Meaning

apare:	=	others
yathayaha	=	of diligence
samsritha vratha:ha	=	of strong determination (engage in)
dravya yajna:ha	=	dravya yajna
thapo:yajna:ha	=	thapo: yajna
thattha:	=	yet
apare:	=	others (engage in)
yo:ga yajna	=	yo:ga yajna
swa:dhya:ya yajna	=	swa:dhya:ya yajna
cha	=	and
jna:na yajna:ha	=	jna:na yajna

Purport

The Lord continues to give a few more kinds of karma yo:gis.

Some engage in using their *dravya*, hard earned money, to donate in charity. Some use it to support temples, while others use it to perform *ho:ma*s. These are some of the ways *karma yo:gi*s

engage in *dravya yajna*.

Some others take extreme vows like cha:ndra:ya:na. They take limited bites of food depending on the phases of the moon. Thapas means denying oneself from sensory indulgence. These people push themselves to take in as little as they can so that they can spend the time thinking about spiritual matters. These are some of the ways *karma yo:gi*s engage in *thapo: yajna*.

Yet others spend their time and energy in visiting places of pilgrimage like Thirumala, **S**ri:rangam etc. and taking a dip in holy rivers. Some preferred to visit spiritual gurus. Yo:ga means *pra:pthi* or associating. Since these *karma yo:gi*s are associating with holy people, holy places and holy rivers, they are performing *yo:ga yajna*.

Some others meticulously study the scriptures as called by their *swadharma*. Those who engage in doing what a *swadharma* requires them to do are performing *swa:dhya:ya yajna*. Finally there are some who practice what they have learnt from the scriptures. Since these *karma yo:gi*s are engaged in acquiring knowledge and practicing that knowledge they are performing *jna:na yajna*.

SLOKA- 29

apa:ne: juhwathi pra:**n**am
pra:**n**e::pa:nam thattha::pare: |
pra:**n**a::pa:na gathi:ruddhwa:
pra:**n**a:ya:ma para:ya**n**a:ha || 29

Word Split
apa:ne: — juhwathi — pra:**n**am
pra:**n**e: — apa:nam — thattha: — apare:
pra:**n**a:pa:nagathi: — ruddhwa:
pra:**n**a:ya:ma para:yana:ha

SLOKA- 30(1)

apare: niyatha:ha:ra:ha
pra:**n**a:n pra:**n**e:shu juhwathi |

Word Split
apare: — niyatha:ha:ra:ha
pra:**n**a:n — pra:**n**e:shu — juhwathi

Meaning 29-30(1)
para:ya**n**a:ha =   Devoted to
pra:**n**a:ya:ma   =   *pra:**n**a:ya:ma*
niyatha:ha:ra:ha   =   (and) controlled diet,
apare: =   some
juhwathi   =   offer
pra:**n**am   =   *pra:**n**a* as *havis*,

apa:ne:	=	into the fire of *apa:na* (i.e. practicing *pu:raka*),
thattha:	=	similarly,
apare:	=	yet others
juhwathi	=	offer
apa:nam	=	*apa:na* as *havis*
pra:ne:	=	into the fire of *pra:na* (i.e practicing *re:chaka*),
apare:	=	some others
ruddhwa:	=	regulate
gathi:	=	the flow of
pra:na+apa:na	=	*pra:na* and *apa:na*
juhwathi	=	(and) offer
pra:na:n	=	various pra:nas as *havis*
pra:ne:shu	=	in the fire of pra:nas (i.e.practicing *kumbhaka*).

Purport

Pra:na:ya:ma is nothing but controlling the breath in three ways :

1. *pu:raka* or breathing in; the air circulating inside our body as breath is called *pra:na*
2. *re:chaka* or breathing out; the pra:na that helps in pushing out the waste from our body is called *apa:na*
3. *kumbhaka* or holding the breath This is one of the eight steps of ashta:nga yoga.

Breath, thought and food are related. Controlling one helps in controlling the other two. karma yo:gis control the quantity, quality, and timing of the food they take. They offer it to the indwelling Lord in the a:thma before taking it in. Thus, they make sure that the food is sa:thwik. This helps them to control breath. As a result, they are able to do these respiratory activities too in a brahma:thmaka way.

Some *karma yo:gi*s practice taking in long breaths. They do *ho:ma* by offering *pra:na* as *havis* into the fire of *apa:na*. Some other *karma yo:gi*s practice breathing out for long. They do *ho:ma* by offering *apa:na* as *havis* into the fire of *pra:na*. Yet other *karma yo:gi*s practice holding their breath. They do *ho:ma* by offering the various breaths as *havis* into the fire of *pra:nas*.

All these *karma yo:gi*s mentioned so far from verse 25 onwards know *yajna*. They know what it is. They know how to perform it. They perform it correctly. As a result, they are liberated from their ka:rmic bondage.

SLOKA- 30(2)

sarve::py e:the: yajnavido:
yajna kshapitha kalmasha:ha || 30

Word Split

sarve: — api — e:the: — yajnavido:
yajna kshapitha kalmasha:ha

SLOKA- 31

yajna **s**ishta:mrutha bhujo:
ya:nthi bramha sana:thanam |
na:yam lo:ko::sthya yajnasya
kutho:nyah kurusaththama ! || 31

Word Split

yajna **s**ishta:mrutha bhujaha:
ya:nthi — bramha — sana:thanam |
na — ayam — lo:kaha — asthi — ayajnasya
kuthaha — anyaha — kurusaththama ! ||

Meaning30(2)-31:

e:the: sarve: api	=	all these
yajnavido:	=	who know *yajna*
kalmasha:ha	=	have their sins
kshapitha	=	destroyed
yajna	=	by *yajna*,
yajna **s**ishta amrutha bhujaha =		eat the nectarine *prasa:dam* of *yajna*,
ya:nthi	=	attain
sana:thanam	=	the eternal
bramha	=	*a:thma* (with the Lord in it);
kurusaththama	=	O Best of the Kurus (Arjuna)!
na:sthi	=	there is no
ayam	=	material
lo:kaha	=	benefit (like dharma, arttha and ka:ma)
ayajnasya	=	for those who do not perform *yajna*;
kuthaha	=	how can they get
anyaha	=	the other (mo:ksha - spiritual benefit of liberation)?

Purport

The Lord clearly points out the importance of engaging in *yajna*. All the *karma yo:gi*s mentioned thus far engage in *yajna*. However, unlike the ignorant, worldly people, the *karma yo:gi*s do not think that they are doing *karma* with their resources so that they could enjoy the rewards of it. Instead, they do *karma* with the knowledge of *a:thma* as *bramha:thmaka*. This liberates them from the bondage to *karma*. Doing *karma* as *yajna*, offering whatever they thus earn as an offering to the Lord, and then accepting that to sustain their body is called partaking *yajnase:sham*. This is *amrutham* or nectar. This helps them attain the coveted, eternal *a:thma*.

Those who do not do karma as yajna do not attain even material success. How can they even dream of attaining the spiritual bliss of a:thma? They will not get that. In Chapter 3, the Lord mentioned that those who cook food for their sake alone do work selfishly for their enjoyment end up in pain. They do not get what they want and become victims to their own unaccomplished desires, consequent anger and fear and envy and so on. This is the pain of samsa:ra. The way out of it is to do karma as karma yo:ga.

SLOKA- 32

e:vam bahuvidha: yajna:ha
vithatha:h brahma**n**o: mukhe: |
karmaja:n viddhi tha:n sarva:n
e:vam jna:thwa: vimo:kshyase: || 32

Word Split
e:vam — bahuvidha: — yajna:ha
vithatha:ha — brahma**n**aha — mukhe:
karmaja:n — viddhi — tha:n — sarva:n
e:vam — jna:thwa: — vimo:kshyase:

Meaning
e:vam	=	thus
bahuvidha:	=	many ways of
yajna:ha	=	performing *karma* as *yajna*
vithatha:ha	=	are explained
brahma**n**o: mukhe:	=	as means of attaining *a:thma*;
viddhi	=	know
tha:n sarva:n	=	them all
karmaja:n	=	to be born of *nithya, naimiththika karma* or related to performing these;
jna:thwa:	=	knowing
e:vam	=	thus
vimo:kshyase:	=	you will be liberated.

Purport
The Lord points out that knowledge is useful only when it is practiced in everyday life. Simply knowing and not practicing it is not true knowledge. Therefore, it is very important to practice what we have learnt from the Lord.

The Lord tells us that our everyday activities, which are of various kinds, can be transformed into *yajna*. They then become many means of attaining *a:thma*. The main thing to note is how to do *karma*. Doing it for selfish reasons, for sense-gratification etc. will lead to binding. Doing it for

universal welfare, for the sake of *a:thma* does not bind.

In other words, when we exploit objects in nature for our selfish reasons, we are doing *karma* that binds. When we enjoy objects in nature as a way to glorify the indwelling Lord of the *a:thma*, we are doing *karma* as *yajna*, and that does not bind us. Eating food without thanking the Lord, creates ka:rmic bondage. Eating food as an offering to the indwelling Lord as a token of thanks, liberates us from ka:rmic bondage. This little aspect of knowledge makes all the difference even though the action of eating food is the same in both the instances.

SLOKA- 33

sre:ya:n dravyamaya:d yajna:th
jna:na yajnah paranthapa! |
sarvam karma:khi:lam pa:rttha!
jna:ne: parisama:pyathe: || 33

Word Split

sre:ya:n — dravyamaya:th — yajna:th
jna:na yajnaha — paranthapa! |
sarvam — karma — akhi:lam — pa:rttha!
jna:ne: — parisama:pyathe: ||

Meaning

paranthapa!	=	O scorcher of foes (Arjuna)!
jna:na yajnaha	=	*jna:na yajna* (see 28 above)
sre:ya:n	=	is better
dravyamaya:th+ yajna:th	=	than *dravya yajna* (see 28 above);
pa:rttha!	=	O son of Pruttha (Arjuna)!
sarvam	=	all
karma+ akhi:lam	=	*karma* in its entirety
parisama:pyathe:	=	culminates
jna:ne:	=	in knowledge.

Purport

We need not worry that the Lord now wants us to pursue jna:na yo:ga. All that He is saying is that performing karma with proper knowledge of how and why it is done is better than mechanically doing it. He is underscoring the importance of jna:na aspect that is an integral part of karma yo:ga.

It is pertinent to recall that karma yo:ga has two components: jna:na and dravya. We know that for karma to be performed, there should be a kartha: or the doer and dravya or the materials involved in the karma. It is the kartha: who has jna:na, not the dravya. It is important for the kartha: to have the necessary jna:na to transform the karma into yajna. A kartha: without this jna:na will not look upon all as brahma:thmaka and cannot transform karma into yajna. As a result, he will be bound by karma even though he uses the same kind of dravya that a kartha: with jna:na does. Thus, the Lord points out that jna:na has to guide the kartha: so that the resulting yajna leads to self-realization.

SLOKA- 34

thadwiddhi pra**n**ipa:the:na
pariprasne:na se:vaya: |
upade:kshyanthi the: jna:nam
jna:ninas thaththwadar**s**inaha || 34

Word Split

thath — viddhi — pra**n**ipa:the:na
pariprasne:na — se:vaya: |
upade:kshyanthi — the: — jna:nam
jna:ninaha — thaththwadar**s**inaha ||

Meaning

viddhi	=	Learn
thath	=	this
jna:ninaha	=	from the wise
darsinaha	=	who have the realized
thaththwa	=	a:thma
pra**n**ipa:the:na	=	by prostrating (them),
pariprasne:na	=	by asking (them),
se:vaya:	=	(and) by serving (them);
the:	=	they
upade:kshyanthi	=	will teach you so well that you can 'see'
jna:nam	=	knowledge of self (a:thmajna:nam)

Purport

The Lord urges Arjuna, and through him, all of us, to reach out to an a:cha:rya so that we too can get a:thmajna:na under the guidance of that a:cha:rya. An a:cha:rya is one who has the a:thmajna:na and knows how to impart it to his disciples. He is a master of both knowledge and practice. He practices what he teaches.

When we approach such an a:cha:rya, we have to be humble, inquisitive, and eager to serve him as he pleases. Humility should come from the depths of our heart. That will happen only when we truly believe the a:cha:rya will help us. Once we are firm in the first quality, we have to make sure that we actually ask humbly for help. We should have the intellectual power to grasp what the a:cha:rya teaches us. All that he teaches us may not necessarily register in our minds right away. We have to wait patiently for the right time and get our doubts clarified. We have to keep serving him out of gratitude as we continue to associate with him. All of this will purify us and re-wire our brains so that we become eligible for the coveted knowledge. The a:cha:rya will make us fit enough for a:thmajna:na and give it to us at the right time.

We might wonder why the Lord asks Arjuna to go to an a:cha:rya when He Himself is teaching Arjuna everything he needs to know. The Lord emphasizes the importance of hearing these subtle spiritual concepts over and over again. Hearing them once may not be enough. Our samska:ras and habits will make us forget even after we hear these once. Therefore, it is crucial to develop humility, patience, and service to fight our previous bad samska:ras and continue to listen to the a:cha:rya again and again until we finally get it.

SLOKA- 35

yath jna:thwa na punarmo:ham
e:vam ya:syasi pa:**n**dava!
ye:na bhu:tha:nya**se**:she:**n**a
drakshyasy a:thman yattho: mayi || 35

Word Split

yath — jna:thaw: — na — punarmo:ham
e:vam — ya:syasi — pa:**n**dava!
ye:na — bhu:tha:ni — a**se**:she:**n**a
drakshyasi — a:thmani — attho: — mayi

Meaning

pa:**n**dava	=	O son of Pa:ndu (Arjuna)!
jna:thwa:	=	knowing
yath	=	that
na ya:syasi	=	you will not fall
punaha	=	again
mo:ham e:vam	=	into this delusion;
ye:na	=	by that knowledge,
drakshyasi	=	you can see
a**se**:she:**n**a	=	all these
bhu:tha:ni	=	ji:vas in various bodies
a:thmani	=	in yourself
attho:	=	and then
mayi	=	in Me

Purport

　　The Lord refers here to that knowledge of self or a:thma, which He had given to Arjuna. The Lord advised us to reach out to the a:cha:rya for further details about its practice. Once that knowledge is ingrained in Arjuna and aspirants like us, we will no longer be deluded by the *ahamka:ra* that "*I am the body*" and the *mamaka:ra* that "the people and objects are *mine to cherish*". We will instead realize that the same pure soul, or ji:va, that is in our body is similar to the ones in all others too, no matter what kind of body we see on the outside. The ji:vas are inherently pure. It is the ka:rmic bondage (strengthened by ahamka:ra and mamaka:ra) that hides the purity. Once the ka:rmic bondage is gone, the equality of all souls becomes apparent. In this liberated state, all ji:vas are equal to each other as well as the Lord in their purity.

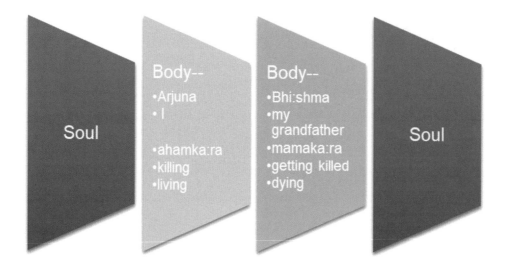

Instead of stopping at the body-level where there are differences, this knowledge will enable Arjuna to go to the soul-level and realize that the souls are similar and have no death.

With this knowledge, Arjuna will not grieve over the deaths of his grandfathers or cousins. He will not consider himself as his body. He will not consider the bodies of his friends and family as friends and family. Instead, he will see himself as a ji:va and others as ji:vas. He will do his swadharma as yajna (without attachment) and he will not be bound in this process.

SLOKA- 36

api che:d asi pa:pe:bhyaha
sarve:bhyaha pa:pakruththamaha |
sarvam jna:na plave:naiva
vrujinam santharishyasi || 36

Word Split

api - che:th - asi - pa:pe:bhyaha
sarve:bhyaha - pa:pakruththamaha |
sarvam - jna:na plave:na - e:va
vrujinam - santharishyasi ||

Meaning

api che:th asi	=	Even if you are
pa:pakruththamaha	=	worst sinner
sarve:bhyaha	=	of all
pa:pe:bhyaha	=	the sinners,
santharishyasi	=	you can cross
sarvam	=	entire
vrujinam	=	sea of sins
jna:na plave:na	=	by the boat of jna:na
e:va	=	alone.

Purport

The Lord highlights the power of jna:na. Even though we have been doing things incorrectly, once we know the correct way, we will no longer do them incorrectly. The Lord gives us a metaphor of a boat and the sea. Even though the waters of sins are deep, we can cross over them by means of the boat of a:thmajna:na.

It is very important to remain in the boat and not in the waters! Similarly, it is important to always know and practice this knowledge so that we don't fall back into our old mistaken ways. In other words, we should not keep repeating our mistakes. Repetition of mistakes indicates lack of knowledge.

SLOKA- 37

yatthaidha:msi samiddho::gnihi
bhasmasa:th kuruthe::rjuna ! |
jna:na:gnis sarva karma:ni
bhasmasa:th kuruthe: thattha: || 37

Word Split

yattha: – e:dha:msi - samiddhaha – agnihi
bhasmasa:th - kuruthe: - arjuna!
jna:na:gnihi - sarva karma:**ni**
bhasmasa:th - kuruthe: - thattha: ||

Meaning

Arjuna!	=	O Arjuna!
yattha:	=	Just as
samiddhaha	=	the blazing
agnihi	=	fire
kuruthe:	=	reduces
e:dha:msi	=	fuel
bhasmasa:th	=	to ashes,
thattha:	=	so also
jna:na:gnihi	=	the fire of a:thmajna:na
kuruthe:	=	reduces
sarva karma:**ni**	=	all karmas
bhasmasa:th	=	to ashes.

Purport

The Lord gives another metaphor. Just as fire burns up fuel, the fire of a:thmajna:na burns up the stock of karma completely.

SLOKA- 38

nahi jna:ne:na sadru**s**am
pavithram iha vidhyathe: |
thath svayam yo:ga samsiddhaha
ka:le:na::thmani vindhathi || 38

Word Split

na - hi - jna:ne:na - sadru**s**am
pavithram - iha - vidhyathe: |
thath - svayam - yo:ga samsiddhaha
ka:le:na - a:thmani - vindhathi ||

Meaning

na vidhyathe: hi	=	There is nothing at all
jna:ne:na sadru**s**am	=	like a:thmajna:na
pavithram	=	that can purify us from sins
iha	=	in this world;
yo:ga samsiddhaha	=	the successful karma yo:gi
swayam vindhathi	=	spontaneously intuits (getting by himself)
thath	=	that a:thmajna:na
a:thmani	=	in his 'self'
ka:le:na:	=	in due time.

Purport

　　The Lord emphasizes that there is nothing as pure as a:thmajna:na in this material world. The karma yo:gi will be purified who diligently practices karma yo:ga as mentioned above and as taught by his a:cha:rya. His tendencies to get attached or angry or envious about material things will drop away. He will become serene. It is a mere matter of time before he realizes the precious a:thma.

SLOKA- 39

sraddha:va:n labhathe: jna:nam
thath paras samyathe:ndriyaha |
jna:nam labdhwa: para:m sa:nthim
achire:n a:dhi gachhathi || 39

Word Split

sraddha:va:n - labhathe: - jna:nam
thath paraha - samyathe:ndriyaha |
jna:nam - labdhva: - para:m - sa:nthim
achire:na - adhi gachhathi ||

Meaning

sraddha:va:n	=	The karma yo:gi who has faith and eagerness,
thathparaha	=	who has diligence
samyathe:ndriyaha	=	who has controlled his senses
labhathe:	=	attains
jna:nam	=	a:thmajna:na;
jna:nam labdhva:	=	having attained the a:thmajna:na, he
achier:na	=	quickly
adhi gachhathi	=	reaches
para:m	=	great
sa:nthim	=	blissful state of peace.

Purport

The Lord mentions the due process of success in karma yo:ga that He referred in the previous verse.

1. The karma yo:gi gets to know what to practice and how to go about it—jna:na.
2. Then he develops a lot of interest in it. He believes that it is possible to attain the goal. He understands how desirable the goal is, so he is eager to obtain it—sraddhava:n.
3. He gets single-minded devotion to it—thathparaha
4. As a result, his interest in other things goes down. He easily controls his senses from running waywardly into the external world—samyathe:ndriyaha
5. His knowledge ripens into a:thmajna:na or wisdom—labhathe: jna:nam.
6. This quickly leads to great, blissful peace —para:m sa:nthim

SLOKA- 40

ajnascha: sraddha dha:nascha
samsaya:thma: vinasyathi |
na:yam lo:ko::sthi na paro:
na sukham samsaya:thmanaha || 40

Word Split

ajnaha - cha - asraddhadha:naha – cha
samsaya:thma: - vinasyathi
na - ayam - lo:kaha - asthi - na - paraha
na - sukham - samsaya:thmanaha

Meaning

ajnaha	=	He who is ignorant,
cha	=	and
asraddhadha:naha	=	who is not eager to get knowledge
cha	=	and
samsaya:thma:	=	who doubts
vinasyathi	=	is destroyed ;
samsaya:thmanaha	=	to the doubter
asthi	=	there is
na	=	no
ayam	=	this
lo:kaha	=	world
na	=	nor
paraha	=	the other world
na sukham	=	nor happiness!

Purport

The Lord warns what happens to those who do not care to get the necessary knowledge to get out of ka:rmic bondage.

1. They neither know nor attempt to learn what is karma or yajna and how to do them
2. They do not believe that it is worth the effort.
3. They have no faith that a:thmajna:na exists or that it is attainable.
4. As a result, they don't get the reward of dharma, arttha, ka:ma in this world nor do they get mo:ksha in the other world.

SLOKA- 41

yo:ga sannyastha karma:**n**am
jna:na sanchanna sam**s**ayam |
a:thmavantham na karma:**ni**
nibadhnanthi dhananjaya! || 41

Word Split

yo:ga - sannyastha - karma:**n**am
jna:na - sanchanna - sam**s**ayam
a:thmavantham - na - karma:**ni**
nibadhnanthi - dhananjaya!

Meaning

dhananjaya!	=	O winner of wealth (Arjuna)!
karma:**ni**	=	*karmas*
na	=	do not
nibadhnanthi	=	bind
a:thmavantham	=	the one who is of steady mind;
sannyastha karma:**n**am	=	the one who gives up all kinds of *karma*
yo:ga	=	intellectually by his *buddhi yo:ga;*
jna:na	=	whose *a:thmajna:na*
sanchhinna	=	has destroyed
sam**s**ayam	=	all doubts;

Purport

The Lord summarizes the main teaching of this chapter.

The *mumukshu* transforms *karma* into *yajna* when he gives up *sanga, karthruthwa,* and *karmaphala:skthi* but continues to engage in *karma* physically. He gives up the thought, "I am doing this for my sake," and this is the way he gives up karma intellectually with his *buddhiyo:ga.* While performing *karma* like this, he gets *a:thmajna:na* that liberates him from *deha:thma bhra:nthi.* So he won't have *ahamka:ra* or *mamaka:ra.* As a result, he is not assailed by doubts again. He knows and does what exactly has to be done. He is liberated from his ka:rmic bondage. Even the past karmas won't affect him in the form of *sukham* or *duhkham.*

SLOKA- 42

thasma:d ajna:na sambhu:tham
hruthsttham jna:na:sin a::thmanaha |
chhithvainam sam**s**ayam yo:gam
a:thish**tt**o:th thish**tt**a bha:ratha! || 42

Word Split

thasma:th - ajna:na - sambhu:tham
hruthsttham - jna:na:sina: - a:thmanaha |
chhithva: - e:nam - sam**s**ayam - yo:gam
a:thish**tt**a - uththish**tt**a - bha:ratha! ||

Meaning

bha:ratha!	=	O descendent of Bharatha (Arjuna)!
thasma:th	=	Therefore,
chhithva:	=	cut up
jna:na:sina:	=	with the sword of knowledge of self (a:thmajna:na)
e:nam	=	this
sam**s**ayam	=	doubt
sambhu:tham	=	arising due to
ajna:na	=	ignorance
a:thmanaha	=	pertaining to the soul
hruthsttham	=	in the heart;
a:thish**tt**a	=	engage in
yo:gam	=	karma yo:ga;
uththish**tt**a	=	stand up!

Purport

Thus, the Lord patiently and explicitly has put forth the karma yo:ga and asks Arjuna to follow it. The Lord has said enough so that Arjuna can stand up and fight the war, having cut off the roots of ignorance about the nature of the soul and body with the strong sword of knowledge.

ithi **s***rimad bhagavadgi:tha:su upanishathsu brahma vidya:ya:m yo:gasa:sthre:*
*sri krush**n**a:rjuna samva:de: jna:na yo:go: na:ma chathurttho::dhya:yaha ||*

ithi srimad bhagavadgi:tha:su upanishathsu brahma vidya:ya:m yo:gasa:sthre: sri
krushna:rjuna samva:de: jna:na yo:go: na:ma chathurttho:dhya:yaha ||

*Thus concluded the 4th chapter 'Jnana Yogaha' of Sri:mad Bhagavad Gi:tha, an Upanishath, a Bramha Vidya, a Yo:gasa:sthra and this is a dialogue between Sri Krush**n**a & Arjuna.*

sri:krush**n**a parabramha**n**e: namaha

sarvam **s**ri: krush**n**a:rpanam asthu

Made in the USA
Monee, IL
18 January 2021

55853695R00036